POSEY TALES
Shirley Posey

STORIES & ILLUSTRATIONS

BY

SHIRLEY A. SCHWINDT-POSEY

POSEY TALES
THE BIG TRUCK WITH A BIG HORN

About Carlyne

Carlyne (pronounced Car-lean) is the oldest of the five Posey children and that proved to be a good thing, since she was definitely born to be a leader, and she could practice her leadership skills on her three younger brothers and one younger sister.

Carlyne was a very energetic little girl. She was kind, loving, generous, curious, and always mothering and befriended every child in the neighborhood. She could make even the smallest of things seem important and exciting. Every day was a new challenge, and Carlyne quickly found some way to occupy her time and the time of those around her.

This book is dedicated to Carlyne

and her family with much love

About the Book

The Big Truck with a Big Horn is about an ambitious, energetic little girl named Carlyne (pronounced Car-lean). She has a great imagination and likes to explore and look beyond her present setting. In this book she wants to see what is beyond the tall grass behind the outdoor laundry room that she imagines to be a jungle. Could there really be real wild animals on the other side?

If not, what is there?

Carlyne's daddy was in the Air Force, and she lived in an apartment building with many other children who also had fathers that were in the Air Force or army

Carlyne was two years old, and she loved to play with all the children who lived in the apartments. She especially liked to play with her little friend, Vickie, whom she called "Giki." They often would play in the gravel courtyard just outside their apartments because there was no large play area for the children.

Sometimes, she would play on the small lawn area in the back of the apartments where her mother would hang their laundry on clotheslines to dry in the summer. They did not have a washer or dryer in their apartment. Carlyne loved to play on the soft grass and take off her shoes. The grass made her bare feet feel cool.

Carlyne also loved to go to the apartment complex's laundry room with her mother and watch the clothes go around in the dryer. She liked to play with the other children in the laundry room.

They would all bring toys to play with. The girls would bring their dolls and girl toys like tea sets and fake food. The boys would bring trucks, cars, and other boy toys like Tinkertoys. It was fun to watch them build things. Sometimes they would share and show Carlyne how to build things too. She liked that very much.

She also liked to look at all the big bushes and weeds just behind the small grassy area and pretend it was a jungle with lots of "wild" animals. Sometimes she even scared herself a little bit when she started to imagine a little too much.

So she would yell, "I'm right here, Mama." Just in case there really were any wild animals in the weeds, she was going to let them know her mama was close by.

When Carlyne played near the bushes and weeds, she could hear the busy highway traffic just a little beyond the other side of the bushes. She was too short to see over the bushes and weeds, so one day she asked her mother, "What's on the other side of the bushes, Mama?"

Her mother said, "There is a very busy highway with lots of fast cars and big trucks and buses, so you must never, ever go any farther than the grassy area. Cars and trucks and buses can be very dangerous if you get in their way, and Daddy and I love you and don't want you to get hurt."

Carlyne's eyes got very big because she was a little afraid, and she said, "I will stay right here, Mama."

But one day, when Carlyne went with her mother to the laundry room, and was playing near the bushes, she kept thinking, "I wonder if there could also be some real wild animals on the other side. I will just take a quick look, that shouldn't really hurt anything."

So, she peeked in the laundry room and saw that her mama was turned away from her, so she said to herself, I'll hurry and come right back. Mama won't even know I left."

Carlyne's mother was about to take her clothes out of the washer when she noticed Carlyne had disappeared. She yelled, "Carlyne, where are you?" several times, but there was no answer, and she became very worried.

Then she heard the terrible screeching of brakes, Screeech, ...choong, choong,... Screeech,... choong,... choong. Then she heard a very loud HONK......HONK...HONK!

Carlyne's mother frantically ran through the bushes and weeds. There, stopped in the middle of the highway, was a great big freight truck, and many other cars that had also stopped. In front of the big freight truck was a very frightened little Carlyne, screaming, "Waa, waa, Mama, Mama! Help! Help!"

The man in the great big freight truck got out of his truck, took Carlyne's little hand, and led her back to her mother.

Then he said, "Little girl, you are very, very lucky that I was able to stop in time and honk my horn to warn other cars to stop, or you could have been hurt very badly. I hope you learned a good lesson from this, and your mama too."

Carlyne's mother picked her up and said, "Well, Carlyne, did you learn something from this?" Carlyne tearfully nodded her head and said, "Yes, I did, Mama." Her mama tearfully said, "So did I." Do you know what that lesson was? If you need some help, see the next page, and Carlyne will tell you.

"Here is what I learned. I learned little boys and girls should always listen to what your mom and dad tell you about what to do and what not to do because they love you and would never want you to get hurt. That's why we have a mom and a dad to watch over us and teach us how to take care of ourselves so we don't get hurt. I never ever went anywhere close to any busy roads again, and when I even just heard a big truck's horn toot, I ran and hid behind my mama."

POSEY TALES

THE DEER BOY

About Monte

Monte is the second oldest child in the Posey family. He was a shy, quiet, and conscientious little boy, with a wonderful sense of humor and a very inventive mind. He would often think of ways to make things to entertain himself or play practical little pranks on family members. Sometimes his ideas and pranks would backfire, but he always, without a doubt, amused the people around him and usually himself.

This book is dedicated to Monte and his family

with much love

About the Book

The Deer Boy is a story about a little boy named Monte. He has a wonderful sense of humor and a creative mind. He has just moved to a new state and is very lonesome for his old home. To make matters worse, his sister is five, and she is going to go to kindergarten and leave him behind. He gets very bored and comes up with all kinds of funny things to entertain himself while his sister is gone. His imagination and creative mind get carried away one day when he sees some tree branches lying on the ground. He thinks to himself, "Hmm,… those kind of look like deer antlers. I could put them on my head and pretend I'm a deer." Now, there is only one problem: how will he get those big branches to stay on his head? Read the story to see how he solves the problem.

Monte was a little three year old boy who had recently moved to a new city with his parents and sister and baby brother.

Even though the new neighborhood had lots of little boys and girls his age, he very often would sit quietly and think of his old home and friends because he was very lonesome for them.

One day he said to his mother, "I want to go back to my home in North Dakota. I think I can walk there all by myself." His mother said, "Monte, did you forget that it took us two days of driving in a car to get here and all those mountains and forests we drove through? The forests have lots of wild animals in them, like big bears and cougars. Did you think about where you would sleep at night when it's dark, and what about food?" Monte's eyes got big and his throat got dry. He couldn't talk for a few minutes, thinking about those bears and cougars.

Monte hadn't even thought about how far away it was, but then he remembered all the mountains with forests. It sounded very scary when he thought about being in the woods alone without Mom and Dad. His mother felt sorry for him when she saw how scared he looked, so she said, "Monte, I have an idea. How about I pack you a lunch and put some clothes in a bag that I will tie on the end of a stick, so that you can carry it over your shoulder? You can go into the small woods behind our house and pretend you are in the big woods and it is night. OK?"

He liked that idea. So after his mother made a sack lunch and put his clothes in a bag, Monte went into the woods, but only a small distance. His mother watched him the entire time from a window. He sat down, ate all the lunch, and then he looked up at the trees and sky and all around. It all looked a little spooky, even in the daylight, so he quickly jumped up and ran back into the house. He said, "I decided that I'm going to stay here with you and Daddy." His mother smiled and said, "Oh good, Monte. I am so happy you decided to stay, and Daddy will be happy too. We love you and want you to be with us forever!"

Monte was happy that he had his sister, Carlyne, to play with because it helped him to get over his loneliness much faster. He liked to wear his Batman costume and pretend he was "Batman", and Carlyne would dress up as "Wonder Woman". Together, they believed they could save the whole world.

Then one day in September, Carlyne went off to school. Monte asked his mother, "Can I please go to school too, Mama?" His mother said, "I'm sorry, Monte, but you aren't old enough to go to school yet. Besides, I would get very lonesome if you left me too. Carlyne will only be gone a short time, and then she'll be home again."

But the short time was a really long, long time to Monte as he waited for his sister to come home from school each day. His little brother, Brad, was too small to play with, and he didn't even understand anything! He would just laugh and squeal when Monte wanted to play.

So, Monte found ways to entertain himself. Sometimes he would play the part of both "Batman" and the "bad guys" and he would punch into the air and roll over and over on the ground, struggling to capture the bad guys! "Take that...and that, you rotten egg!"

Sometimes he would make a kazoo with a comb, paper, and a rubber band and pretend he was playing in a band.

Sometimes he would even make an airplane with combs of different sizes and fly high above the skies to lands far away. He found all kinds of ways to entertain himself.

One day he really became creative! His mother was busy with his little brother, so he asked her, "Can I go outside and play for a while, Mama?" His mother said, "Yes, Monte, and remember, play nice and don't get into anything you know you shouldn't." Monte said, "OK, Mama, I won't," and he happily ran outside to play.

Monte's mother had just put his brother, Brad, down for a nap when the phone rang. It was her next door neighbor, Mary, and she was laughing. She said, "Shirley, you just have to look out the window and see what Monte is doing, but don't let him see you because it's too funny."

So Monte's mother peeked out the window, and there was Monte, pretending he was a deer. He had found some tree branches that looked very much like deer antlers and had taped them to his head with almost an entire roll of masking tape. He was bounding and jumping around as if he was fighting or playing with another deer.

Monte's mother laughed to herself. Mary was right! It really was a funny, funny sight, but how in the world was she ever going to get those tree branches off with all that masking tape on his head and hair?

Monte's mother let him play and pretend for a little while longer since he was having such a good time. Then she went outside and said, "Are you having fun, Monte?" Monte replied, "Yes, Mama. Watch me run and jump. I'm a big strong deer like Bambi's daddy."

Monte's mother said, "Well, yes, I can see that, Monte, but did you ever think about how you were going to remove those tree branches with all that masking tape stuck to your hair and head?" Monte thought for a while, and all he could say was "Uh-oh, I didn't think of that!"

Monte's mother had to work for a very long time to get all of the tree branches and tape off her son's head. She even had to cut some of his hair off, and he already had a crew cut. The tape did not come off easily. It pulled some of Monte's hair out, and his head really hurt. Monte's mother said, "Well, Monte, did you learn a lesson from this?" Monte said, "Yes, I did, Mama." Do you know what that lesson was? If you need some help with the answer, see the next page and Monte will tell you.

"I never had such a sore head ever again. I learned a good lesson. Don't ever use masking tape to tape something to your head. It sticks really good, especially to hair. Always ask your mama to help you if you want to make something stay on your head. She knows better things to use. Anyway, I didn't need a haircut for a long time!"

POSEY TALES

THE BURNING BROON

About Bradley

Bradley (or Brad) is the third Posey child. He was a loving, generous, and happy little boy, with a smile so big that his almond-shaped eyes would almost close. He liked to give and get lots of hugs and kisses.

 He was a very busy little boy, whose chubby little legs ran all day like bicycle wheels in motion. Because of his constant movement, he was by no means easy to keep up with and would often get into mischief, which required extra hugs and kisses for reassurance that he was loved.

This book is dedicated to Bradley and his family

with much love

About the Book

Bradley is an ambitious three year old boy. He is always looking for action and excitement. He is a very busy boy, constantly on the move, and by no means easy to keep up with. In *The Burning Broom,* he loves to watch his mother burn paper in the outdoor brick barbecue/incinerator. He likes to throw in a few sticks and leaves once in a while, but the sticks and leaves aren't exciting enough. He decides to toss in something bigger that really burns nicely. A broom! His mother scolds him, and he promises never to do it again. Will he or won't he? What do you think?

Bradley was a blond-haired, blue-eyed three year old boy who was always looking for excitement of some kind or other. He loved to play with his older sister, Carlyne, and his brother, Monte. Sometimes Carlyne would pretend she was his mother and dress him up to look like a baby.

Bradley liked that because Carlyne and Monte would pull him around in the wagon and pretend it was a stroller. That was a lot of fun!

Bradley also liked to play with the family kitty, who was named "Tatty", because his fur was nice and soft and he purred when you petted him. Bradley also liked to listen to him meow, so sometimes when his mother wasn't watching, he would swing him around in circles by his two front paws. Then he really meowed a lot! Bradley laughed because it sounded so funny when the kitty meowed so loud.

One day, Bradley's mother heard the kitty meowing a *loud* meow like he was in pain. She ran into the living room, and there was Bradley swinging the kitty in circles. His mother scolded him and said, "You are hurting Tatty when you swing him by his front legs, and that's why he meowed so loud. You could break his little legs. You wouldn't want that to happen, would you?" Bradley said, "No, Mama, I'm sorry. I won't do it again."

Bradley kept his word for several months, but when Carlyne and Monte went back to school in the fall, he didn't have anyone to play with except the kitty, Tatty. One day Bradley's mama heard Brad and Tatty both making loud, desperate noises. The kitty was meowing loudly, and Bradley was crying, "Help, Mama, help. Tatty won't let go!" His mother came running into the room, and Bradley was right. He was holding Tatty, and Tatty had one of his claws stuck inside Bradley's nose and would not let go. His mother finally got the kitty to let go.

Bradley was never going to ever let that happen again. That really hurt, so he decided to be very good friends with Tatty. Bradley was going to be nice to him so he would never do that again. He would sit and hold him and pet him very nicely.

One of the things that Bradley probably liked to do most was watch his mother burn paper and milk cartons in the outdoor brick barbecue pit. It was fun to watch the paper crumble and turn into flames. He liked to run around and find little sticks and dry leaves to throw into the fire and also watch them curl up and burn.

His mother was a little worried because she saw how much Bradley liked to watch the fire, so she explained, "Fires can be very dangerous, Bradley. They can burn you very badly if you get too close. Fires can even burn down houses if you're not careful. So don't ever go near the barbecue pit unless I am out here with you."

Even though Bradley listened carefully to what his mother said, he still wanted to play with some of the fire. One day, after his mother had set the trash on fire in the brick barbecue pit and took him back in the house with her, Bradley grabbed his mother's broom and quickly ran outside and threw the broom into the fire.

Bradley's sister, Carlyne, and brother, Monte, saw him throw the broom in the fire and quickly ran into the house to tell their mother. "Hurry, Mama. Bradley threw your broom in the fire, and it's burning all up!" Tatty, the family kitty, seemed to smile when he heard Bradley might be in trouble.

Bradley's mother was very worried but happy when she saw that her son was OK. But the broom was not so OK, so she was a little angry. It was all burned, and she would have to buy another one. She told him, "See that broom and how it's all burned? Well, that's just how little boys who like to play with fire can get burned. Now, you go to your room and think about what you've done. I'm happy you are all right, but never do that again."

While Bradley sat in his room, he thought about what his mother had said, and he remembered how fast the broom burned. Could he really burn like that broom? It made him a little sick to think he might look like the icky black broom if he got burned by the fire, so for a long time he was a very good little boy.

But after a couple of months, Bradley's little mind forgot all about what his mother had said. He just wanted to see a broom burn again one more time. So one day when his mother was burning some papers in the barbecue pit, she took Bradley back into the house so she could finish some work she had started. Bradley saw she was busy, so he quickly grabbed another broom, and ran out the back door, and threw it into the fire.

This time, his mother heard him go outside, so she quickly ran out the door after him. Bradley was still hanging on to the end of the broom when his mother came out, but the straw end already had started to burn.

When he saw his mother, Bradley became frightened and excited and pulled the broom out of the fire and threw it over the fence. That was a very bad thing to do. It hadn't rained for a while, and the grass was very dry, so the entire field behind their house and the neighbors' houses started on fire. His mother said, "Oh no, Bradley, now just look and see what you've done!"

It was a good thing all of the neighbors were home and saw the flames. They all came running out to help Bradley's mother and dad fight the fire. They brought old blankets, old coats, and rugs to beat out the fire. Bradley felt very bad as he watched them and cried very hard. He was worried someone might get burned or maybe even his house could get burned like Mama had said.

After the fire was out, Bradley's mother and father asked him, "Well, Bradley, did you learn a lesson today from everything you saw and did and all the trouble you caused us and the neighbors?" He said, "Yes, Mama and Daddy, I did, and I'm so very sorry."

Do you know what that lesson was that Bradley learned?

If not, go to the next page and he will tell you.

"I learned that fire can be very dangerous. Little children should never play with fire. It can burn down people's houses and even burn people. I never ever wanted to watch my mother burn our newspapers and milk cartons anymore. I didn't want to see any more open fires either. I really got scared when I saw the fire get so close to my house and our neighbors' houses. Always listen when your mom and dad tell you what NOT to do so you won't hurt yourself or other people. I think maybe they must have learned some lessons, too, when they were little."

POSEY TALES

DRYER'S AREN'T USED TO DRY ANIMALS

About Kirk

Kirk is the fourth child in the Posey family. He was a quiet, happy, loving, and funny little boy. He loved animals, especially baby kittens and puppies.

Kirk also loved to sing songs and tell stories to himself while trying to fall asleep during nap time and at bedtime. Some of his favorite songs included ones you're all familiar with, such as "Rudolph the Red Nosed Braindeer," "Lacoodalda-Coodalda-Rautcha," and "The Wobblin Goblin with the Broken Broom." The neighbors would pay him a quarter just to listen to him sing, and for a quarter, he would sing his heart out!

This book is dedicated to Kirk and his family

with much love

About the Book

Kirk is the fourth child in the Posey family. He is a happy, loving boy who likes to sing and make up songs. He also loves animals, especially kittens and puppies. In *Dryers Aren't Used to Dry Animals*, he tries to get his parents to let him keep a kitten that he says he found close to his home. He wants them to think the kitten followed him home. It is a summer day, and he opens the door and tries throwing the kitten into the house, but before he gets the door closed, the kitten runs outside again. He finally succeeds after several attempts and tells his parents that the kitten ran in when he opened the door. The kitten causes more trouble than he had anticipated. Does he find the owner? Just how does it all end?

Kirk was born into a family with one older sister and two older brothers. His brothers were very happy to have a new baby brother, but his sister, Carlyne, was a little disappointed because she wanted a baby sister.

The first time she looked at Kirk, she said, "I didn't want you; I wanted a baby girl." Her mother heard her and said, "Oh, you'll make him feel bad. Look how cute he is. He doesn't even know he's a boy, and he's so happy to be here." Her mother's remarks worked. Carlyne smiled and said, "I'm sorry, baby. I love you anyway."

When Kirk grew a little older, his brothers, Monte and Brad, taught him all the important things boys need to know about, such as Batman and Robin, Superman, dinosaurs, how to climb trees, and even how to catch a ball—and how *not* to drop it!

His sister, Carlyne, added a little of her motherly touch. She played house and pretended he was her baby, just as she had done with their brother, Brad. *And* she taught him how to sing songs.

Kirk would sing himself to sleep every night and roll his head from side to side with the music. Sometimes he would make up songs. His entire family liked one he made up about a frog. They would often stand outside his bedroom door and quietly listen to him sing, "I went to a pond and what do you think I saw? I saw a little-froggie that's what I saw. He looked at me and said, "Hi, Kirkie, and I said, "Hi, froggie, I came to listen to you croak." And the froggie said, "Then I'll croak. Croak, croak, croak."

One night, Kirk saw his family because the door was open, just a little, and right in the middle of his "Froggie" song, he pointed his finger at the door and said, "Don't peek." Then he kept on singing his song. They all looked at each other in surprise and laughed softly because they didn't know Kirk had seen them.

Besides singing, Kirk also loved animals, especially baby kittens. The family already had a dog, Skipper, and a cat named Tatty, but almost every day Kirk would ask his mom and dad, "Please, can I have a baby kitten? I would take very good care of it." The answer was usually the same. "We already have a dog and a cat, honey, and that's quite enough."

One day when Kirk asked again for a baby kitty, his mother said, "Well, Kirk, honey, besides already having a dog and cat, you also have a big problem with fleas biting you. Just look at all of your flea bites. If we got another kitty, it would be twice as bad, and your dad and I don't know what to do to make the fleas stop biting you." Kirk looked at his mother and said, "I know what you could do. You could buy me a flea collar."" His parents laughed and explained that flea collars were only for the animals, not for humans.

Kirk didn't mention wanting a kitty for a long time. Then one nice summer day, his parents heard the front door open and close very fast several times, but no one came in. When they looked out the window, they saw Kirk talking to a little black and white kitten. In a nearly tearful, desperate voice, he said, "You stupid kitty! Now, when I open the door and throw you in, you stay in. Don't come running back out again!"

His parents turned to each other with puzzled looks on their faces that seemed to say, "What is he doing?" Just then, Kirk picked up the kitty and threw it inside the house again and quickly, but awkwardly, ran in behind it, slamming the door before it could run outside again. Much to his mother's and father's surprise, he shouted, "Mom…Dad…look what ran inside when I came in the door!"

Even though Kirk's mother and dad felt sorry for him, knowing how much he wanted a kitten, they explained that this was someone else's kitty, and he could not have it because some other boy or girl would be very sad if their kitty did not come home. So they would have to try to find the kitten's owner.

To make matters worse, they had just moved into a new home and didn't know the neighbors' names or phone numbers, so they had to go door-to-door in the neighborhood trying to find the owner. They didn't have any luck finding the owner, but they did get to meet many new neighbors who became their friends.

Kirk's mother said, "The kitty will have to stay outside on the porch overnight. Maybe it will try to find its own way home. If we bring it inside, it won't be able to look for its home." And the next morning, the kitten was gone. It looked as though it had found its way home.

By afternoon, however, it began to rain, and as Kirk looked out the window, there on the front porch was the black and white kitty, all wet from the rain. Kirk was very happy and excited to see the kitten and ran outside to give it a hug.

Kirk's mother was in the kitchen baking cookies, so he thought she might not notice if he sneaked the kitty into the house and dried it and played with it for a while.

All at once Kirk's mother heard the clothes dryer running and a loud
"THUMP, THUMP… MEOW!" THUMP, THUMP… MEOW!" She quickly ran
to the laundry room to see what was going on. When she opened the
dryer door, out came a very dizzy, cross-eyed kitty. His fur was standing
on end, and he was meowing *loudly* as he ran, zigzagging very fast to find
the open back door. Kirk's mother tried to catch him, but she couldn't find
him.

Kirk was standing nearby with a terrified look on his face, saying, "Sorry, sorry!" His mother said, "My goodness, Kirk! You could have killed the little kitty. *Dryers aren't used to dry animals.* You are very lucky I heard the dryer running." Kirk said, "I didn't mean to hurt the kitty. I only wanted to dry him so he wouldn't catch a cold." Of course the kitty never came back, and Kirk learned a valuable lesson that day.

Do you know what that lesson was? Go to the next page to find out.

"I learned that kittens cannot be put in the dryer to dry them, and I should not have sneaked the kitty in without my mama knowing it. She said she would have helped me dry it with a towel and tried to help me find the kitten's owner again, but I wanted to keep it and hide it. My mama and daddy were right. I should not have tried to keep someone else's kitty, and besides,… I got a lot more flea bites!"

POSEY TALES
BUBBLE TEARS

About Toni

Toni is the youngest of the five Posey children. When Toni was born, her father asked the school to excuse her brothers and sister so they could go with him to bring her home. The love and bond they developed that day continued throughout her growing-up years. Toni never wanted for love and attention, and because of this, she developed into a loving, happy, and confident little girl. She loved dancing and gymnastics, and in her later years, she won several ribbons and trophies in both. Toni was matter-of-fact and to the point when speaking, which made her a funny little girl. Toni will always be known as "our" baby to the entire family!

This book is dedicated to Toni and family

with much love

About the Book

Toni is the youngest of the five Posey children. She never wanted for love and attention. Her four siblings adored her. She was a cute and busy little girl with curly blond hair, who required a watchful eye or three!

In *Bubble Tears*, Toni tries to help her mother with housework, without Mother's approval. It looks like so much fun. She has some toys that are used for cleaning, but she wants to try real furniture polish and real bathroom cleaners like Mama uses. She does indeed try to advance to washing her own hair. Is it all really more fun? Check it out and see!

Toni was the youngest child in the family, with one older sister, Carlyne, and three older brothers, Monte, Bradley, and Kirk. When she was born, their dad called the school and asked them to please excuse his children so he could take them with him to pick up their mother and their new baby sister from the hospital. They all were so happy because none of them had a baby sister before.

Toni was born in December, and the entire family thought she was the best Christmas present ever! When she woke up at night, her sister and brothers also woke up and argued about whose turn it was to hold her. Their mother decided she had more help than she needed and was thankful Toni slept all night at an early age!

Toni's sister and brothers never tired of playing with her as she grew older. They got excited over every new thing she learned. They liked to make up funny nicknames for her and laughed when she answered to them whenever they called her by those names. Some of the funny names they called her were Pumpkin, Tonelda, Gootschmear, Mrs. Beasley, Toni-Roni, and Dumpling. She answered to all of them. Her sister, Carlyne, would call,"Gootschmear, where are you?" And she would say, "Hewe I am."

Toni loved the family dog, whose name was Whiskers, but she couldn't pronounce the last part of his name ("kers"), so she called him "Whiskey." Whiskers liked to play with her because, even though he was a dog, he knew she was a little girl and needed someone to play with and watch over her. He was a good watchdog.

One day when Toni's mother was busy ironing clothes, Toni decided to visit her grandma all by herself. Grandma lived real close, only half a block away, *but* Toni would have to cross a road to get there. She rattled the doorknob until it opened, and off she went. Whiskers ran out right behind her. When she tried to cross the road, he barked loudly and ran back and forth in front of her, so she couldn't cross. Toni's mother heard him and ran outside. She was so happy Whiskers had stopped her. She gave him a big hug. Toni's dad bought a new lock for the door, and that never happened again.

Toni was a quiet little girl until she was two years old, and from then on, she was not so quiet. It all started about a week after her second birthday, around December 16th. Her mother had just wrapped all the Christmas presents and put them under the Christmas tree when she heard Toni singing "Happy buthday to me, happy buthday to me, happy buthday to Toni, happy buthday to me."

Toni's mother was working in the kitchen. When she heard her, she went into the living room to see what she was doing. She found Toni opening all the Christmas presents under the tree. Her mother explained to her, "These are not your birthday presents, honey. They are Christmas presents, and we have to wait for Christmas to open them." Toni didn't understand, but Mother did convince her to *not* open them until she told Toni she could.

Toni liked to watch her mother clean house, and very often she would try to do some of her own cleaning, just like Mother. She liked to sweep the kitchen floor with her little toy broom and pretend she was sweeping up dirt in her little dustpan.

One day she decided to dust the coffee table, just like her mother did. She sprayed the coffee table with furniture polish but didn't bother to remove anything on the table.

She said, "Look, Mama, I powlished for you." But her mother was not too happy with the polish job. She said, "Oh no, Toni, that is not the way we polish furniture. See how you got furniture polish on my doilies and nice things on the table? We only polish the table. It's nice that you want to help your mama, but I will show you the right way to dust when you get older."

Another day, while Mother was vacuuming, Toni decided to clean the bathroom. She dumped two bottles of strawberry shampoo and hair conditioner into the bathtub and mixed it all around the bottom and sides of the tub, really good!

Then she dumped a half can of Comet cleanser in the sink and on top of the counter, and used lots of water and a washcloth to scrub it all around. "Now dis weally looks clean," she told herself. "Mama will be happy." But...

Mama was not so happy! She said, "Oh no! Toni, Toni! What a mess you have made. Shampoo and conditioner are for your hair, not to clean the bathtub. The Comet can be dangerous, as well as most cleaning things. I don't want you to get sick or to hurt yourself, so please, let Mother and your sister do all the cleaning, and you wait until you get older." Toni said, "But it smwells so clean in hewe, Mama."

In the months that followed, Toni tried very hard to do pretend cleaning only, but it wasn't as much fun. She remembered how nice the strawberry shampoo smelled, so one day she said to herself, "Maybe if I use it to wash my hair instead of the bathtub, Mama won't mind so much." So she stood on the toilet seat cover, leaned over the sink, and dumped the whole bottle of strawberry shampoo on her head.

Her mother was working in the kitchen when she heard a loud cry for help. "Mama, Mama, help, help! Ow, ow! Waa, waa!" Her mother ran into the bathroom and found Toni covered with shampoo suds and screaming because the shampoo had run down her face and into her eyes. As she was crying, the tears coming from her eyes formed little bubbles from all the shampoo in her eyes.

Her mother quickly rinsed the shampoo out of her eyes with clear water until real tears streamed down her face and no more "bubble tears" appeared. After calling the eye doctor to make sure no damage was done, she hugged Toni and chuckled a little about the bubble tears. She asked Toni, "Did you learn a lesson from all this, sweetheart?" Toni, with very red eyes, replied, "Uh-huh, Mama, I did." Do you know what that lesson was? If you need help, go to the next page and Toni will let you know.

"I learned that I should always let my mother wash my hair until I get older and know how much shampoo to use. I know that you don't need a whole bottle of shampoo to wash your hair. You should always listen to your mother when she tells you to wait until you get older to help with housework too, because like my mama told me, some cleaning things can be dangerous. The Comet made my hands shrivel up, and I don't ever want any more shampoo in my eyes. They really burned. I don't really like 'bubble tears' either."